MW00561978

FIREMAN

COLORING BOOK

SPEEDY
PUBLISHING

1112

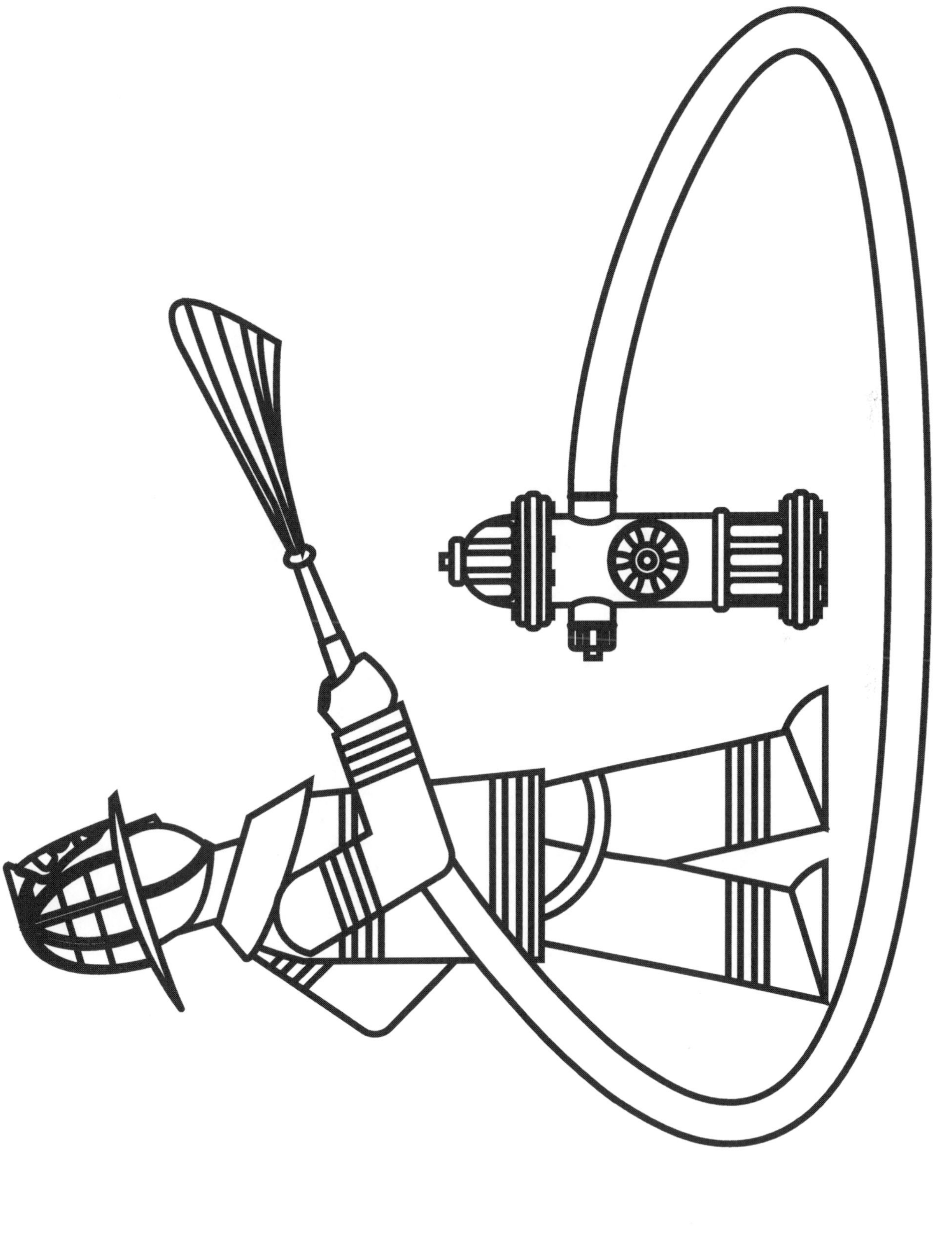

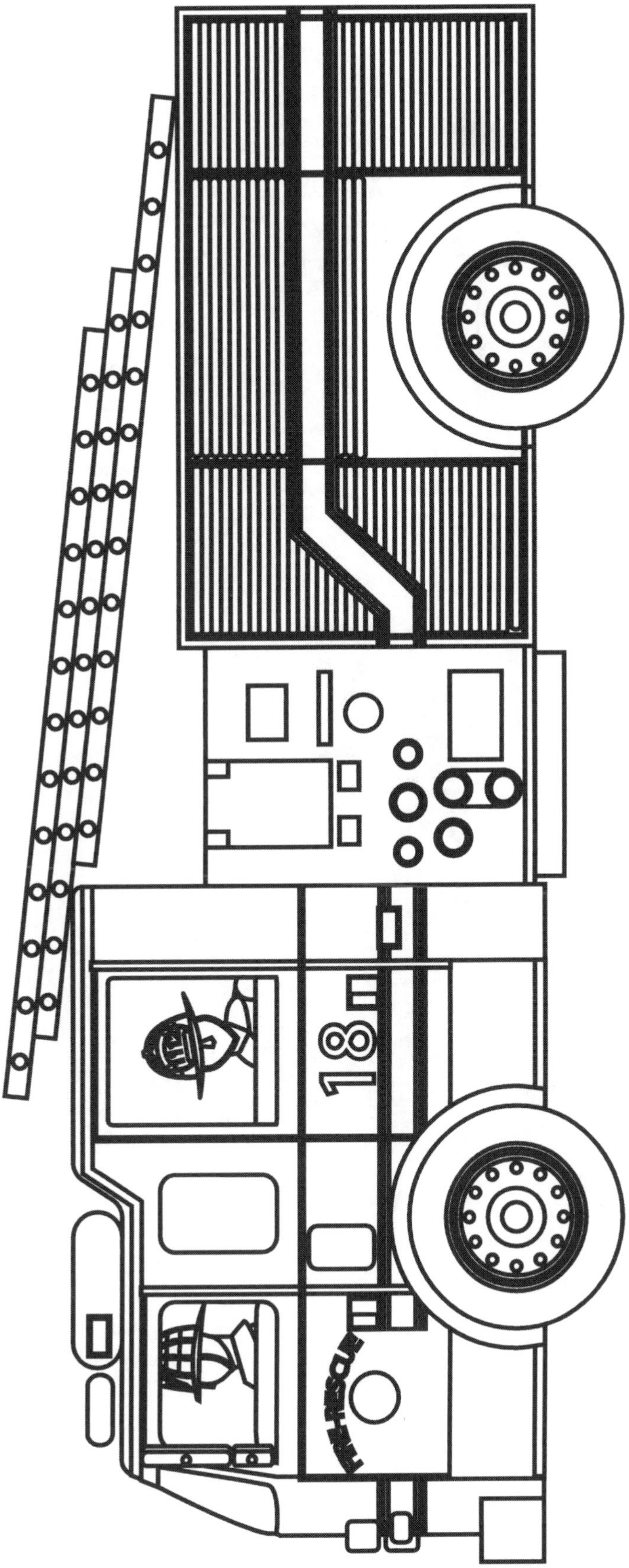
18

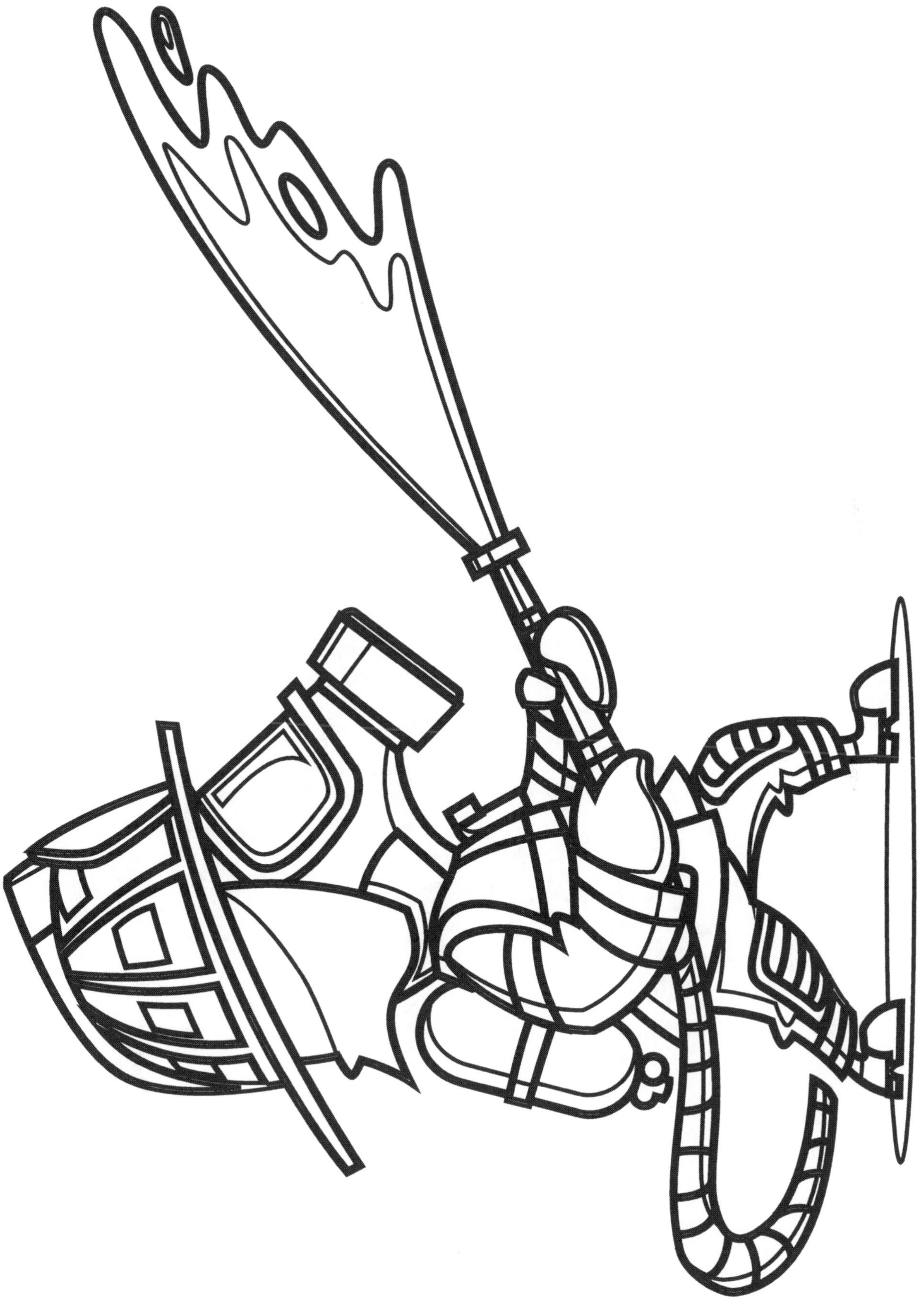

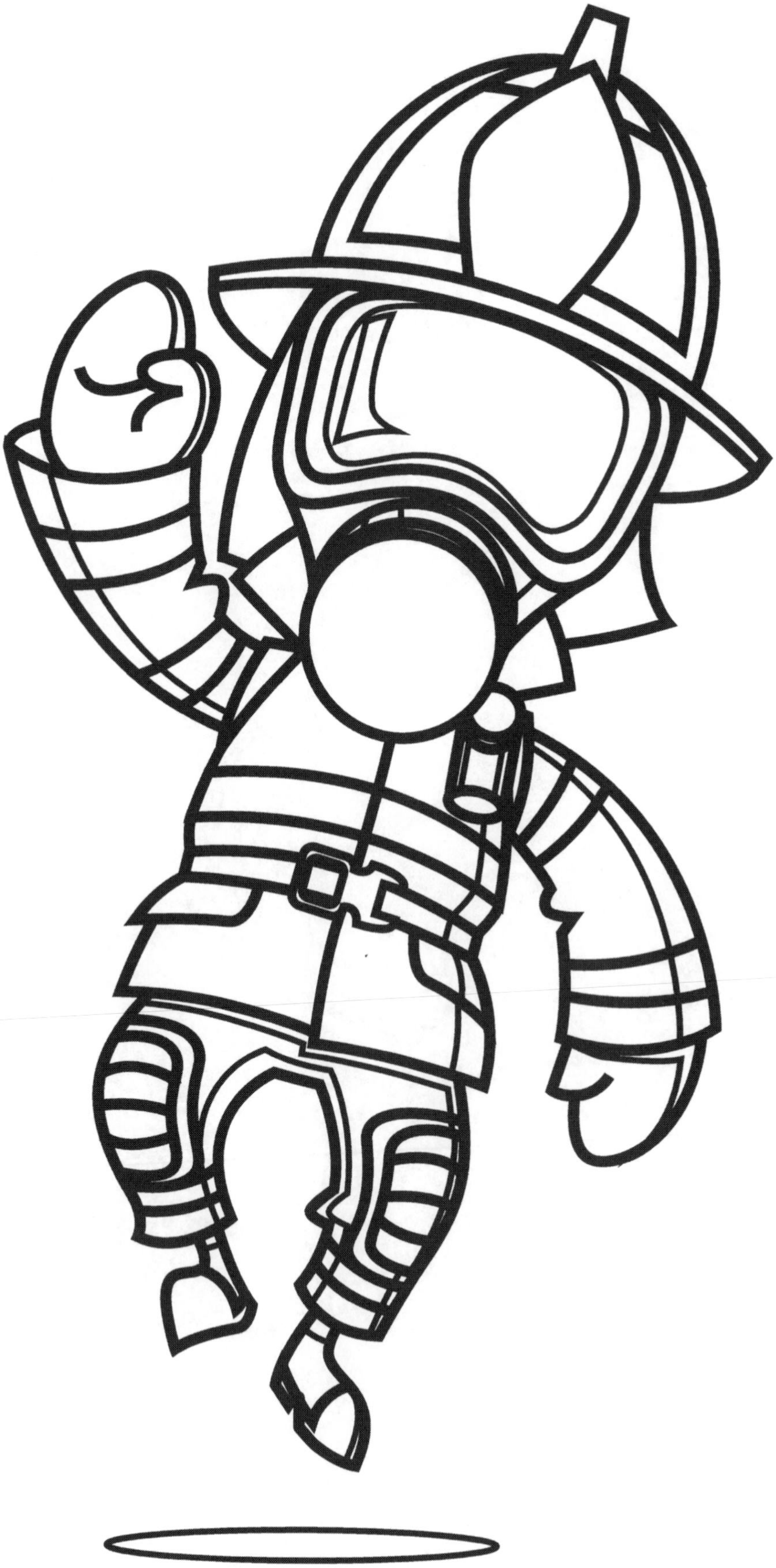

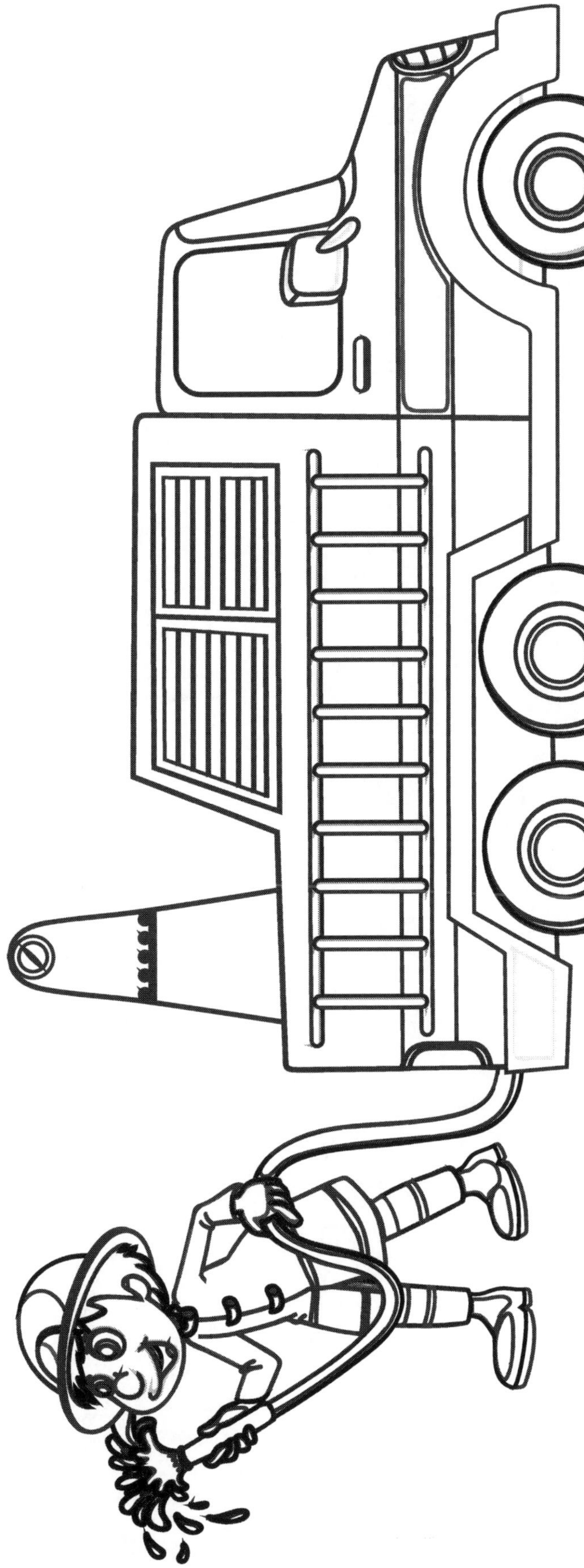

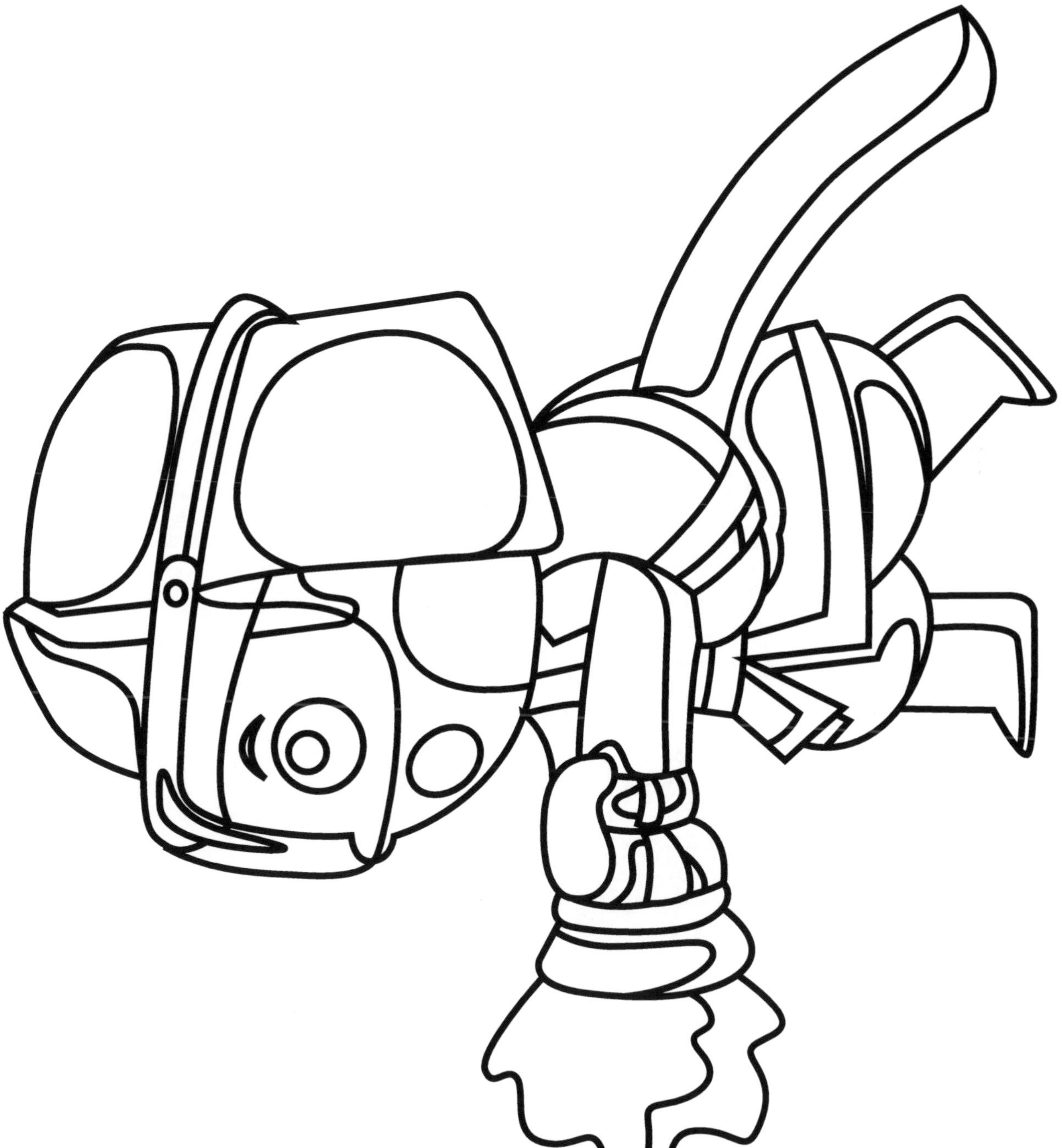

59362288R00020

Made in the USA
San Bernardino, CA
04 December 2017